Alert to Glory

Alert to Glory

by Sally Ito

TURNSTONE PRESS

Alert to Glory

Turnstone Press
Artspace Building
206-100 Arthur Street
Winnipeg, MB
R3B 1H3 Canada
www.TurnstonePress.com

Turnstone Press gratefully acknowledges the assistance of the Canada Council for the Arts, the Manitoba Arts Council, the Government of Canada through the Canada Book Fund, and the Province of Manitoba through the Book Publishing Tax Credit and the Book Publisher Marketing Assistance Program.

Cover design: Jamis Paulson
Cover art: Gen Tsuboi
Interior design: Sharon Caseburg
Printed and bound in Canada by Friesens for Turnstone Press.

Library and Archives Canada Cataloguing in Publication

Ito, Sally, 1964–
Alert to glory / Sally Ito.

Poems.
ISBN 978-0-88801-379-8

I. Title.

PS8567.T63A64 2011 C811'.54 C2011-903245-7

MIX
Paper from responsible sources
FSC® C016245
FSC www.fsc.org

Contents

Alert to Glory *is, above all, the fruit and labour of the soul,*
and therefore dedicated to God,
with whom the soul most richly desires communion.

Alert to Glory

Eye, The King

Alert to Glory

to sun-break and water-burst, to land-ho and pinnacle reach
to shimmer shine of light on wave, of moon glow on broken glass;
to face-praise the world in the stroll-hours of the park; to hear
the lark music of argument in the pew wing of the fowl;
for before anywhere, it begins in the *seeing*, alertness before the glory
in the bit sound of hammer pound, from the spark and spray
of smithies in the watery forge behind the eye
where tears spring like iron to shoe the horse of sight's delight;
alertness, the soul's beam, light tunnel of praise, through which
to gain-gallop the cup, the trophy,
the thing won and earned by having been sought and found,
Glory, the lost sheep of Joy.

Apprehend

To handcuff the world, make it prisoner to sense and scrutiny.
To apprehend. That is the poet's task. The lonely jailer
seizing at the company of things. Not to possess or own
but rather to perceive the world like a nerve quickening
to touch, or a flank quivering to the wind. To apprehend
is surely one of God's commandments to the steward, that poet,
who in his hour as policeman might enjoy the brief moment
of a world in fetters for him. Catch-and-release—the finny,
slippery silver underneath the hand—is the currency of joy,
the fine paid for the alertness and watching which is the poet's
constant state. He apprehends, and the world is seized
and God makes wonder of his heart.

The Dominion Is Wonder

You have given them dominion over the works of your hands;
you have put all things under their feet.

—Psalm 8:6 (NRSV)

The dominion is wonder
and eye the king, the glassy orb
        on throne of flesh and bone
that partakes of the hour as if
        feasting on time, every season a victual,
a morsel of delight, savoured
and then remembered.

No power, no lust in this,
        sheer appetite for the world,
the inescapable greens and blues,
        palettes of ether and water,
into which to dip the eye's
        brush-tip, as if in broad stroke
the eye might possess the canvas the way
        a portrait does, face conjured
from out of cloth and wood.
His face, smoked mirror to our own.

Ordinary Awe

Awe came upon everyone. Ordinary awe, the kind that filters
through the fog of everyday. Shaft of sunlight on plant,
slip of birdsong when suddenly motes are illumined, and
random notes form a chorus. Ordinary awe, the grain of sand
in *potentia* for the mirror, the glass, that vessel that may hold
the image, wine that is wondrous, divine. Such moments
when the mind-bell is struck dumb and the hollow fills
with shuddering sound, come once and once again.
Ordinary awe compels as suddenly as it recedes
—a wave that enters, sweeps away, sometimes returns.

Sparrows

Today, He is in the sparrows
in their ruffled ordinariness
on the back fence, picking
at leftover seeds and fruits
of the dead. In winter,
the sparrows bear the burden
of the cold, light as the cross
of their hollow bones, and
from the window, they are,
in the glare of holy every day,
framed and hallowed prayer.

Sunspit

Can a mote in the eye be pure light?
Sunspit, for example?
Happiness that stings the sight
until it bursts into tears
—fountains of severe delight?

God, the peashooter, the honey hurler
of joy,
unexpected.

Could insult be ever so delicious
as spit from the lips of divinity,
spirit distilled from pure essence?

Give me the mote that so blinds with joy
that nothing might cause me
to judge or be in want ever again.

Give me sunspit to rub, rub in the eye.

Clouds

The heavens are telling the glory of God; and the firmament proclaims his handiwork. Day to day pours forth speech, and night to night declares knowledge.

—Psalm 19:1, 2 (NRSV)

Hopkins kept a diary of cloud movements, noting their varied shapes
cirrus, stratus, cumulus, nimbus—words of Latin origin—profitable for the
observer on the ground who might also think—heap, layer, curl, strip.

Poet purveyor of the sky, head cocked back
has eyes only for the ancient text of the heavens
wherein 'firmament proclaims' and 'day to day pours forth speech.'

Who knew the sky contained so much of Him?

The atmosphere is a book of His declarations.
Like the dew that saturates the ground, the words leave a residue,
minute blessings, wet almost as rain, forming beaded necklaces
that garland the lashes, sight's pearls.

That knowledge can come this way from a gleaning of the fields
that in between white furrow and furl might reveal seed
that bears blossoms and new fruits of wonder,
articulate as the lines that make up the edges of petals
on the surfaces of a drawing—
these are the arts and meats of contemplation that make up the poet's hours.

Trumpet

On 20th-century composer Charles Ives' orchestral piece "The Unanswered Question"

It is not used here to herald a king or announce heaven.

No, heaven *is* the subtext,
a harmonious background, sublimely indifferent—
the white page of a score on which the bleat of a trumpet
is the blundering path of a black fly
drowning in the milk of the universe.

Such exquisite query! How forlorn its echo
in this maw of the cosmos!

It transcends—

a triumph as immeasurable as the vast nothing of sense
which churns out the music of its spheres in response;
first, in grandiose indifference, then in blithe, impatient reply
—a shrill hail of cacophony

to a question only and always,
unanswered.

O Magnum Mysterium

On 16th-century composer Tomás Luis de Victoria's "O Magnum Mysterium"

It is called "sacred polyphony"
this—the true voice of God returned;
        the babble of praise, sung up in strains,
a harmony that braids and twists its ropy voice
        back to heaven.

What have we only but this?

For the cord with its blood feeds us, too;
its chorus of cells   humming, breathing, singing
with the pulse quickened in it
by love.

Alleluia, alleluia, alleluia!

to the mysterious force that through a rope of flesh
connects us to the dark, wide heaven above.

Poems for Advent: A Series

The weeks of Advent are marked by themes. The contemporary themes are Hope, Peace, Joy and Love. The traditional themes were Death, Judgement, Heaven and Hell. These poems are juxtaposed meditations on both themes.

On Hope and Death

It is impossible that anything so natural, so necessary, and so universal as death, should ever have been designed by Providence as an evil to mankind.

—Jonathan Swift

The old hope *was* for death. The promise of heaven a release
from the unremitting hell of life on earth. War, famine, disease—
Life's rack on which to stretch the breath to its last shuddering sigh
was always promised an end. *God is faithful, God is nigh.*
He will not suffer you more than you are able.

What is hope then? Mostly, a scalloped heart of waiting,
a bruised flesh of wing awaiting deliverance, remembering flight.
It is about singing to bide the time and losing oneself in the song.
Death comes sweetly to some, cradled in night's old charm
of lovers meeting, but this time of Creator with created.

Hope for death is no blind thing, but sight lucid with anticipation
fixed on a distant shore as good as anywhere, and mostly
good for just being there as death, inevitably, is.

On Peace and Judgement

With good judgement comes peace, this much is true.
But there are different kinds of peace—
ceasefires, uneasy truces,
peace-at-all-costs, and peace-above-all.
Since we cannot always have our cake and eat it, too
we must often settle for the lesser kinds
and the rumbles they leave in the stomach.
This time, the promise is of flesh—flesh to bear its name,
flesh to be pierced, bled and dried
so the hunger of our disgruntlement
may be met for all time.

If only it were so. If only in eating and drinking blood
we could settle all scores,
forgive and forget, be merry and celebrate.

Good judgement when meted out is all about festive peace,
but bad judgement cries out for more.
Barabas, Barabas, it says,
for there is nothing like the present to muddy eternity,
nothing like giving up a god in exchange for a thief.

On Joy and Heaven

If heaven is joy, and joy heaven, where might we find it here?

Rare glimpses, distant sightings are all that permit of heavenly joy.
Like the way we gaze on dense lights of stars millions of years away
visible only because of an alignment of time and season.

Ah, but to actually *live* in such a star, burn away a self
that knows only temporal happiness and no more.

It is earthly joy—intermittent bliss and spark—that alas,
awakens us to the eternal, and our own condition, finite,
resting like a ball on a flat edge before the abyss.

We are given joy because we are given death. And Heaven
will be its name until we arrive and know the true end of time.

On Love and Hell

Love is Hell, an old song goes, piped in the crushed gravel tones
of a sot who has known too much of its woe. Lovers who have
met the boot, or booted themselves, know the pain love costs.

Like Dante's Hell, there's a special ring for each earthly affection—
love turned to jealousy, turned to rage, love turned to adultery, love
turned to hate. Deeply fallen into the well of our own disgrace,
we cannot make true *caritas* of God's gift without the rings
of our flesh binding us. There's sometimes too, just plain
hard-heartedness, the *I don't love you anymore* indifference
to sacrifice and giving, even of a god of his very life.

Beneath the cross, commerce and junkets still prevail, and love,
love from up there must look like Hell.

The Kingdom of Forgive

Father, forgive them for they know not what they do,
sayeth the Son, and in the Kingdom of Forgive,
these are the words for the people who commit
"the evil that we do"; words for the blunt-nosed herd
bludgeoning the shepherd.

For the Kingdom of Forgive is about abandonment—
abandonment by the flock of him, and him by the Father.

Such loneliness!—the expanse of every parable
spread over the heart like a blanket of ash. How desolate the cry!

Who are they really, these sheep? These fetid creatures born
to bleat, blare, bruise the head? They cannot hear;
the cloven hoof is in their yellow eye, and they are
deaf to words. Forgiveness will not touch them.

But yours as always is a kingdom—generous and beyond
understanding—and they who do not recognize you,
work, alas, as assassins for the King.

Spring Break

Spring break. Kids are on the loose in the mind and everywhere.
Down by the creek, they club the ice with thick branches,
pelt its surface with stones, crying *die, die, die.*
Geese honk overhead in couples, or ragged threesomes,
forming loose patterns in the sky.
The wind is bracing, making cheeks apple red.
Crucifixion is in the air, winter on a cross,
and the children with their clubs, boots and stones
spit at and taunt the dying god, stabbing at the old
wineskin hide in want of something better.
The oldest child has broken off a slab of ice as huge
as a continent and it floats on the cold gummy abyss
freed from the fetters of the land that claimed it.
Now ice returns to the form it once was, as the
god who took on flesh returns to his—*spiritus,*
the world now forever altered by his having been in it;
—altered now as the landscape is when we partake
of its transformation as he partook in ours.

An Easter Devotional

Winnipeg, Canada

Spring here attends You
with rude violence,
snow-melted blight exposing
brittle arrows of trees, barbed shrubs,
sodden ground littered with last year's toy or shoe—
a testament to the wasteland of the heart
before the warm blast of breath that bursts
open the pod, unclenches the fisted bud.

The river rumbles, ice breaking into jagged slabs
thundering and carving its way through—
now flooding the plain, now grinding down
the beds of stone beneath its weighted flowing.

Bread left out for the birds,
sopping with spring sleet becomes a sponge
for the wine of Your thirst
or in the same day in the dry heat of a sudden sun
a crust so hard it is the stone
that cries out Your name.

How spring here lays bare its naked terrain
in remembrance of Your dying flesh,
its vein soon to rupture too, with the blood
of new life, to seep in at the edges.

The mourners still in their winter overcoats,
boots laden with the mudcake debris of last year's leaves,
tramp past Your cross, hushed with lowered eyes
to a ground tarred and dark with death.

They will await the coming season
like the old woman at the kitchen window
straining to see the sky stitched
with the jagged V of returning geese,
harbingers of the season like the unravelled linen
trailing the path in front of the opened tomb.

Creator Destroyer

And God said to Noah, "I have determined to make an end of all flesh, for the earth is filled with violence because of them; now I am going to destroy them along with the earth."

—Genesis 6:13 (NRSV)

Hopkins burnt his poems before entering the Order,
so too, Rouault, his paintings. Gone, lost, irretrievable.
Soul corrupted; now everything must be destroyed.
Still, the heart is an ark. It holds the stomp, bite, chafe
of hooves and fur, the hooded gaze, the stinging tail
—everything that was created, more or less—to survive
predators, bitter foes, enemies, even the Creator Himself
on a rampage. Like the hacked-off faces of stone saints,
the soul gazes eyeless at the destruction, self-less in its daze.
Meanwhile in the wood, the floating bark, some remnant
of mercy sharpens tooth and claw to bound across the plain,
soon to emerge under the coloured archway.
The eye, washed of itself, will return to its face
to draw once more from the inkwell of the earth,
the palate of the seas, visions in a season new as spring.

Spring

Everything is pain, even the green liveliness
that afflicts the bones in spring.
The jerk, twitch and tic of it, the restless
fit of flesh bursting out its bud,
is like a joint knuckling out its skin
in some damn accident of happiness.

Some say the dead will rise like this,
skeletons out of the earth's caress
rising like stems and stalks, firm as pillars
of the faith they once were and no less;
ascending out of the bath of death
clothed in matter, they are still weightless
but dense with grace that dews with heaviness
foliage, strange and lovely, eerier to bless.

Hunger and Innocence

Sister Candida

(St. Benedict's Monastery, Winnipeg)

I am here for spiritual direction.

In a chair outside the director's office,
I await the appointment by reading a book
on the history of the order.

Sister Candida's picture is on page forty-five.

In the middle of a Manitoba winter
in the years of the Depression,
Sister Candida, dressed in her habit, holds a rifle.
Around her, children, charges of the order,
display her catch:
three dead rabbits on the snow.

They will eat well tonight.

When the director ushers me in,
she asks me why I have come.
I tell her it is all
about hunger and innocence:
the quickening of white in that
obscure dazzle of snow,
the need to aim and shoot,
the way Sister Candida does
to feed the orphan heart
the flesh and blood of love.

The Cloister

Before entering,
let me have my spring,

I say, in that last wistful glance back
at the world,

but having tasted the sweet snow once,
the thirst for it never ends.

Why this cold longing
for love that is dead?

Do you not know that winter still burns for spring—
that beneath sheets of glimmering white
are hidden the seeds of paradise?

Slip back the cover   and
reveal the lover never always there
who sleeps with you in the cowl of the habit,
in the shorn and haloed head of prayer.

This melancholy longing,
so barren   so desolate   so beautiful

is a burning, too

that will set the snow aflame
and blaze white the trail to heaven.

At the Beginning of Lent: Ash Wednesday

My mind is a brick and nothing gets through; the porous sponge
of my youth is desiccated into a slab of stone.

Painting the ashes on such a surface is an idle act
or a leap of faith by the bestower;
for the mind while receiving this mortal dust of sacrifice
is wandering through the temple maze of sellers
wondering what to buy, eat in the morrow.
Well, there'll be no sugar, caffeine, or even meat.
The beans will need soaking, and the fish bought fresh.

The sermon is about a recalcitrant camel
made to suckle its mutant offspring,
an oversized albino calf whose onerous birth caused the mother's
heart to harden, become indifferent. My mind is that heart.

The shepherds hire musicians, sing and rub the poor mother's neck,
and finally, teardrops glisten in that old *naga*'s eyes and she is made
to look on her child as if it were her own for the very first time.
The brick now sodden with tears
will keep in the moisture longer than you think,
and when through the doors of the church I slip into the world
the ash will be in me like salt in the sea.

Bisque

After hearing of the death of Margaret Avison,
you have a dream. You are with her in a mountain town
she recollects from her young womanhood. You are
walking down a road. She is looking for a house
—"bisque-coloured," she says. (*Bisque* is a word
that would have found favour with her.)
She once lived there.

That old town is gone, you think, but
some things are still there, like the big sign
for a hotel, shaped like a star. It had some words
on it. You recognize that sign;
you read about it once in her poems.

Everything is bathed in a golden light
—of a time more innocent, bygone. You think
you are travelling back with her
when in fact, she is leading you to the heaven
she remembers poetry was for her;
she is returning to the bisque-coloured house
she once lived in. She is showing you
the end of poetry, the end of a line in time.

Poetry

for T.B.

It is a discipline of consciousness, the poet said,
to see the bruise of blue between the stars,
to link time, and measure through its loops
the certain destiny of words.

The practice of it is as ancient
as the tides of breath
that warm the shores
of our sleeping, dreaming selves.

We cannot wake without it whetting our lips
—a balm for the mortal in us that
ventures out into the gall of day.

We wait for it, attentive,
even though it is the birth room of the heart
where the misshapen stone, the follies of our fallen selves
become breath, words
small and radiant
as the stars that would guide us into heaven,
blue's final end.

Caress

On Sundays, from the back pews of the church,
hands are visible. They stroke the necks of wives,
play with their hair. The hands belong to the married
or to the newly-just. For them, such touching is permitted.
But for the gaze of the one without, the pew is a lonely perch
from which to survey the vast landscape of love. Like a hawk,
hungry for God, lonely for His touch, the sight is quickened
by all that rustling in the grass. If only in the dark corner of prayer,
He might come with His hand, Master of the Hunt,
so that you might swoop down on it and feel His fingers
stroke the down of your breast.

Grapevines

Grapevines are vigorous and forgiving.

The Concord on our back fence is a riot of vines,
each one furling out like a tentacle into the air.
Clamouring for a hold onto anything,
their reach is blind. My art is the same way—
constantly seeking, groping for elements
to sustain it—light, air, water.
No fruit grows here; only wild misjudgement
that thinks more arms to flail
will somehow better hit the mark.

Here then, advice from the experienced:

"Hack, hack away!"
"If it looks like you pruned too much, you didn't."
"I once ran over the vine with a lawnmower, and the
next year it produced the most fruit we had in years."

How can fruit be produced from the bruised nub
of one's effort, cut off at the pass, by forces
as ruthless and indifferent as, well, a lawnmower?

There is blood in the vine that is shed
each time the blade meets it. And from that blood,
forgiveness, and stranger yet, vigour.

It is a mystery.

I am the vine, ye are the branches: He that abideth in me,
and I in him, the same bringeth forth much fruit: for
without me ye can do nothing.

Poets out of Stones

God can make poets out of stones. And He has.
Witness this one. Grey, smooth and round,
it fits into the palm nicely, the way an egg would.
And here, too, is the jagged one, glinting with
bloody garnet, or take this chalky one, crumbly
but still there even after scraping and dusting off.
Everyone is a poet that is stone wanting to cry out.
Yet their words become bread crumbs no one eats,
snippets of song no one hears, and yet,
they still cry out. *Hear me, hear me!*
For these stones do not praise God,
no, even though He has made them.
How perverse this generation!
Who shall read their works?

Poet

I don't think about art when I'm working. I try to think about life.
—Jean-Michel Basquiat

I've had it all wrong these years
trying to make a career out of skipping stones
on the smooth flat waters of the lake.

The quick, shapely thrust of the arm
was all it was worth to me,
and the distance the rock could go.

That unruffled calm on the water was God's indifference,
or even my own, perhaps. Who knows.

How I craved for something to come out of a stone
smacking the water!

Applause, and then some.
Some deeper satisfaction.

Words to burst the stillness, words that leapt
and played the soul like a drum.

Poetry.

Is that all it is? Is that all I am good for?

Titanic

A poem about literary ambition

As a boy he was obsessed by the facts of the disaster,
read books about it, watched documentaries.
In adolescence, he began to write of it tentatively—
a poem here and there, a survivor's tale, a drowned person's lament.
The drama was simply too irresistible, called out for art.
In the future he hoped to write a play, no, better yet,
a screenplay, because he knew every little detail of the incident;
he was an expert. But then came the movie—a blockbuster,
record-breaker at the box office—fully a disaster for him
who had nowhere to go with his dreams, no one
to be his agent, producer, director. In short, no one
who could manifest his vision.

Sometimes some of us will be swallowed by the maw
of a yarn so big, we become Jonahs inside of it, small
and insignificant, angry. What then were we escaping
when we walked up the gangplank onto a vessel doomed
by its own hubris? Jonah, what can you tell us, the failed
artist sitting in the darkness?

Self

Self.
The grit and glitch of it.
That dithering, doubtful spectre haunting the threshold,
motes unable to cross into the light.
It trails you, stitched to the heel and boot of you,
a shimmery sheath of particles, not yet a cape
by which to wing yourself to heroic heights.

You climb a tree, thinking to get away from it,
and it climbs up after you, never far behind,
always wanting somehow to be with you,
beside you, inside you.
A penny for your thoughts? it says.

Unable to discern your face from its own, it seeks
to make the dust it is, one with the flesh you are.

Boomerang

With a poem I am given a phrase. Often when I least expect it. When my mind is on something else. And my hands busy. Yet it must be caught at once, for it comes like a boomerang riding a magical arc, and continuing its forward path, it will vanish unless intercepted.

—P.K. Page

I've lost it again
whatever *it* was—
the light that informed
the bones of my thoughts,
that cast like a sizzle onto the wall
an x-rayed imprint of skeletal truth.

The joints exposed
are the shape of boomerangs
that swing through the dense electric air
to be caught by the momentary meditative mesh
the mind finds itself in occasionally
when glancing out a window
or at a plant or at some white domestic space
like the refrigerator door or the back of an envelope.

If only the joints could cease
their feckless turnings and tossings.

If only the bare, wooden bone
of pure message
could distill in the mind
the *liquor sweet of poesy*
that had all time to savour itself
and not this half moment of
recollected sensation only

twisted regret
over words long gone
disappeared into the white vagaries
of unrecorded time.

Lost Day

When the children don't have school
for some reason or another, or there's been an accident
or some matter that needs your attention RIGHT now
and the day you think you had is suddenly gone,
where does it go in your absence?

It, too, needs a holiday and will whisk itself from under your feet
to bask in its own escape from your purpose, your unremitting will,
your addiction to its usefulness.

The birds that held your glance only moments ago
now trill the loss with fervour, and you, for once, must submit.

At Dusk

The blind man and his companion
are out walking on the street.

The blind man's white cane
is cocked just-so in the crook of one arm,
not that he needs it now—
but soon, at any moment, he must be prepared.

The other arm he has linked around his companion's.

The sun begins to set—daylight's inevitable fall—
when all that is around
merges into murk and blur of darkness.

It is the companion now who enters
the terrain of the blind man.

Together, they proceed,
the only reality between them now *felt*
—as in the rub of the sleeve or the nub of an elbow,
that sturdy, hard circle of skin where flesh and bone meet.

The nudge away or towards,
the brushing, the glancing off, the slight prod—
all that is given on this walk
is sufficient, somehow.

Armaments

He makes wars cease to the end of the earth; he breaks the bow, and shatters the spear; he burns the shields with fire.

—Psalm 46:9 (NRSV)

He who strings the bow must break it.
He who sharpens the spear must shatter it.
And he who forges the shield
must melt it.

Only he who makes the weapons
can destroy them, finally.

Weapons for glory seek victims to hunt down
but this one lies down already.
Bespeckled and camouflaged, its innocence is an infant's.

Its only hope is in a hand stayed, a hand that
in wielding wood, metal, stone, might find glory
        for once, in mercy and adoration
to what will soon rise out of the hidden glen
ethereal but incarnate, before its swift and sudden
flight into heaven.

God the Tea Master

All the weapons we marshal to confront the day,
You ask to be left by the door before entering.
The sword in its sheath must lie on the grass,
the quiver and bow hung off a branch.
Daily mind, that dons the armour of thought,
does not shed the weaponry easily; too many are the tasks
that require its particularity—its thrust-and-jab conquest
of the hour, the arsenal of muscle-and-aim,
to kill one after another, disappointment,
discouragement, or to dent the thick underbelly of despair.

Confronting the day requires such armaments.
But You do not. Even the most shallow practitioner
of Your art is welcome into Your teahouse.
And You serve, as always, grace.

In the quiet sipping, the hours become an eternity,
a night of waxing and waning moons
in contrast to relentless day.
Naked and unarmed, the infant to its mother—
this is the way You would have us come
to You and be served.

Broken Things

Those who find another use for broken things
are saints. The chipped teapot for a planter, a cracked saucer
for its bottom, the torn dress become clothes for a doll
—all converts to another life from the hand that rescues.
Thrift, some call it, that compulsion to save everything,
to still make it useful, but I call it grace—the way a person's life can
sometimes be resurrected from the ashes of suffering or loss—
to gleam through crack, chip, or tear
in hands that do not abandon.

Little Gidding—In Homage

April 1999

Why have we come this way like Eliot,
searching the purpose in a walk meandering between
two distant poles of learning, Oxford and Cambridge,
having no matter but the substance of our will
determining each step?

Is this a calling, then?
Or some old wound that needs bathing
with the salt of tears to make it smart again?

Is the way for knowing only that you know?

They call it "testing your vocation";
to hear only as God hears prayer,
to hear the innermost request of the heart
to serve.

*

The dead here walk in splendour
and have forged the bones of old belief—
an iron horse of working memory.
Engines of their effort still remain,
churning out steams of breath
indicating life.

The chapel is freshly swept, walls marked with words
that still move this secular century's poker-faced observer.

There are new buildings now,
meeting rooms, a library, a parking lot
and two caretakers, old and tender as the light
that fills the recently built rock garden
scented with herbs the Ferrars would have known.

There was a community here. Once and once again.

*

Either you had no purpose
Or the purpose is beyond the end you figured
And is altered in fulfilment.

What sleeps most in the ardour of belief
is the memory that *all* has been believed
once and yet once again

in that space between
the "little while" and the "not yet"
of His coming.

We must still continue
dreaming our destinies into being
with the small furnace of our faith,
the engines of our will.

*

Our feet crunch on the gravel back to the car,
bags stuffed with postcards, pamphlets.

We are not sorry we have come.

The *husk of meaning* is still intact;
if, at all, it was there to begin with,
we will not know
'til, in turning back,
we remember with glory
the moment He was there
and we were gone.

The Spiritual Gifts: A Series

Now concerning the spiritual gifts, brethren, I would not have you ignorant...
—I Corinthians 12:1 (KJV)

Wisdom

Wisdom, not air! Can anything harden the flow
and drift of time into the glassy gem? Wisdom
should be such a stone, itself contained
as the diamond air is between drawn fingers and fisted bow.
(Still, the image is *trajectory*.) Even if into the past, the arrow
goes and stops the young buck's heart, it will have broken through,
made its purpose known. And the air that wisdom was,
the diamond, will have closed its mouth half shut
and like a weir at the river's narrows,
will have caught its prey, the pleasure of the hunt
its quiet and ultimate endeavour.
No, Wisdom moves; it will not be still and will pursue its prey
as the air covets the mouth that speaks it
and delivers it without measure.

Knowledge

But how like chatter it is, as fine dust to its pebbled kin.
Wisdom, it is not. Dins and cacophony of thought
like the racket of newspapers and dance floors,
aswirl with baubles and bons mots, tidbits of gossip,
morsels of ideas for the thinker in a festive mood. And yet
it has its purpose as layers of dust that mark time always do,
preserving the remains of some light-boned creature of the air
long gone, extinct now but for the imprint there.

The whispered page can thus, in turns, become profound
when Knowledge, slight and willing, takes the floor.
For in the seasoned hand of time, grace becomes that paramour
joined things in love sometimes become, a union for eternity,
the dancer to the partner, conjoined, one, as pages
of experience are in the books of the wise.

Faith

Bricks of water, mortar of the ocean, foundation deep;
of substance but of no shape; a dwelling for the teeming millions
in the shallows, a desert of steep vents and caves in the depths.
Vastly present and everywhere palpable;
liquid and viscous, it fills veins and arteries, floods the channels
and summons strangers to its banks. What mystery then
except the eye be clouded with too much of it, soured into belief
by that tart prick of a thorn into sight's flesh? True grief
finds no solace in it but must bathe in its essence, and emerge
a new creature, born again out of the salt of its wounds.
Such are the creeping things that slither out of there;
soul of fin and scale made bold
by what has shaped it and shapes it still—
trickle, runnel, deluge that fills its veins
and yet makes it hunger after air.

Healing

In that forest of crutches by the church door, laid by those
who know best that even walking is an act of faith
is a dim pathway, dark and cluttered with the sin of hoping
too much. Here, the crumbs that litter the floor are stones.

The children lose their way and do not know where to go.
They eat those stones in hope for more. Now a witch lies
in wait for them behind the candied stone and archway—
the witch of Siloam who with spit and mud will cleanse
the eye to restore hidden sight made blind
by a self sore with want, crippled with need.

Cross over the threshold then, fall into the pool already there,
fall in amongst the bones and skin and hair
of all the others who die, rise, and fly—innocents of the air,
now cherubs, from the dross chamber of flesh that chains
the hungry witch to her pool, that stokes
the fire of faith for a share of its bread.

Tongues

Music, is it not? Bubble-bursting babble cracking open reason,
laying bare the heart beating there, tune thrumming through veins
in that just-revealed life in the shell. First music, akin to the feathered limb
still wet with birth, and of no use until flight is in its season.

Scoff at the man swaying in the aisles, Greek froth at his lips and you laugh
at yourself, at the blade of bone stuck out the back like a worn-out nub
in a body old with the ground. You too were an angel once, no stranger
to trill and flight; you flew up to the rafters and sang by halves

in languages distant as the sun. Remember? Tongues are like that:
mysterious vibrations of the mouth's muscle—seething shill
to reason, cheeks in chatter, tooth and jaw aflap in white water
readying the wing always there, readying it for the distant and flat.

For some, the tongue will always be just a fool flap of flesh, literal
like the chomp and chaw it is nestled between, never to be vibrato
in the chambered rafters of praise and glory, but like a limp shrug
at words it never owned, chained to the ground by doubt's hard metal.

Interpretation

Tongues' twin to confusion, we want its glassy presence in the mirror.
For all that is given is "but to see things darkly"; no face to face with Him
made into flesh, the meaning shaped into matter as all things interpreted are.

We will have our mysteries clarified much as we are able, as light into bands
through glass makes colour, name what we cannot grasp nor hold in hopes
for more of that music which has no words, no shape, no sound, no body.

Some though will still look askance then at the babble that confronts
and will not want meaning from it, for what is that to them? Or us?
Tongues mean nothing then and are better that way, easier to deride, dismiss
as one fell swoop of the hand might hit a bird in flight. And still miss.

Speak intelligibly about the mysteries, or so the apostle says, speak and let
the coal go out into the air, and watch for it to blacken there as ecstasy
smoulders itself into meaning—the common ash of reason and good sense.

Discernment

How to part the waters, when water is the tool? No pry, hook, or point
on this blunted instrument of knowing. Sometimes it is the vision
that needs priming, and with the grease of tears, some things are mended,
it's true. But refining decisions to clarion tones so lucid light shines through
is bone out of joint in the human scheme of things.
Still we muddle along, picking apostles with straws,
praying for rain in the eye to take shape there,
a lens to sharpen the sight on that round and milky orb,
itself a chamber of flaws—home of beam and mote,
stem and stalk of sawed-off light.

How then take the inner world and reflect from its broken sense
the strength and will of purpose driven by the engine of the sun
and make of its solar heat, pure storm, a gale willful and intense?
What in a billion miles of darkness will have its run
at the eye and like all unusual weather, make the eye to pause
and consider the moment of its own seeing, unique and temporal as a tune
that brightens the hour? Epiphany. We wish for nothing but sight's laws
conjoined—seeing and seen made one, discernment, the boon.

Claimed for a Season

Ducks

Of plastic or rubber, they are fixtures
around the tub. Daughter plays,
floating them on the shared pond
of our bathing as we splash together—
two birds in the shallows.

You are the mommy duck, she declares,
planting the largest one near the stretch-marked plain
of her birthing, *and I am the baby!*

The smallest yellow one is launched,
   bobbling, nodding, quivering
towards me.

All the nested down
of my wings stirs
not for flights of imagination
but for the shape of this smaller self
returning to its mother

whose body,
once melting with the skies,
has now been claimed for a season
by its young.

Pull Toy

... therefore I will put my hook in thy nose ... and I will turn thee back ...
—Isaiah 37:29 (KJV)

My daughter likes to leash things—
teddy bears and inflatables
dolls and bags.

Pulling them along after her,
she exhorts their cooperation:

Come now! Here we go!

Dragged along the ground after her,
the objects are nonetheless—obedient, compliant.

I remember the feeling well.
After a bad patch in life, there was such a time, too,
when I was pulled by the words in a book,
and from "whence I came, did go back."

Once, my son pulled me by the hand through a labyrinth
painted on a church basement floor.

Come on, Mom, he urged. *Don't worry, we'll get out fine!*

Pull-toy. The soul on a string.

Is this what it means to be led by a child?

Puzzle

You are one, child
like the one you are presently solving on the floor.
One piece, connecting to the other—or not—
making a picture of the whole.

Where does this go?

Your guess is good as mine.
We solve together.

As the pieces join to form the image of a farm
with its red barn and tractor,
penned pigs and flapping fowl,
I wonder who knit the joints of you in my womb

that nameless being you once were then,
cells like jigsaws multiplying and connecting
one to another like this picture emerging
out of the collected effort of our will.

The sheeps go here, right, Mommy?

The satisfying click of that last piece,
the lamb by its mother under the shade of a tree
does not escape my scrutiny,
my gratitude.

Ball

The ball with no name on it is lost.

War has broken out among
the neighbourhood children.

You took it!

No, I didn't.

The girl who grieves its loss the most
claims it was hers.

It was a gift to my parents when they were married,
she says absurdly. *They never played with it, so it's mine.*

The girl is an only child.

Somewhere the ball lies hidden;
it is taking a break.

It will never be owned by anything
but the air, and even then, only temporally

the way a child might inhabit the heart
for a moment before growing up.

Making Cakes

And Abraham hastened into the tent to Sarah, and said, "Make ready quickly three measures of choice flour, knead it, and make cakes."

—Genesis 18:6 (NRSV)

The husband commands thus, and she obeys, compliant wife.
Make cakes. Her belly is a cake, flat and unleavened.
All these years, trying. Husband hanging on fool promises.
Taking flour, water and oil, she kneads and punches.
Slappity slap. Whap, whap, whap. *Make cakes he says,*
she grumbles. For whom? Outside are three strangers,
black shadows from behind the tent flap. She hears their voices
between the whaps and slaps of bread being pounded out,
bread like flesh, bread she will feed to nameless beings
her husband has once again deigned to entertain. Through
the other flap, she sees husband dragging the calf across
the yard. He will slaughter that creature for them, the madman,
always so hasty with the killing. Crazy old coot.
Ah, but she has loved him. Whap, whap, whap.
Who else but a crazy man would stay with her
who cannot bear children? She is finished.
The round, flat cakes are done, waiting to be baked.
And then she hears a voice say, *Where is Sarah?*
She looks up. Why, they know her name!
She thinks and laughs. Laughs at the one her husband believes a god.

Cherubim

They are the true children of God:

gilded and golden
but too often
undusted, chipped and forgotten
in some dark corner of the church.

These wee children abandoned
like old jewels in a mine
have come to resurrect me.

Their seduction is perfection:

round apple cheeks
curly twists of hair
chubby arms and legs

beckoning me into that hunger
that grows steadily
like the rounded orb of the rising sun
that first nibbles the hilltop, then feasts
on the grassy flesh with a light that consumes
dazzlingly   the body,
the whole of it, filling the appetite
with sudden conception,
a child.

See those three by the Holy Mother?

They swoop down from the altar,
come at last to claim me
as *their* mother,
these orphan children of God—
who draw out my love for Him,
with their golden bows, their jewelled eyes,
their cupid laughter.

Pregnant Again

With this second child,
the dreams are more intense.

Twice, I have met with the dead,
conferred with them
for suitable names

which I cannot remember
on waking.

*

In my prayers
        the names swell
on the periphery of my vision

like the image in the side mirror
of the car behind getting bigger

that is all of a sudden beside me
in a blaze of colour and light

passing like a comet.

*

Consulting old books with mythic figures
or family genealogies or even the etched names
of gravestones

doesn't stir up what was lost, once remembered—

the name floating above the fire—
indiscernible, a charcoal cipher on an
ashen sheaf.

*

In the final dream before the birth,
I turn and ask
the one I will not let go

What is your name?

And the answer will be:

Why do you ask?

And as reluctant as a lover,
I let go,
wrestle with the blessing
about to emerge,

nameless, beloved.

Clematis

It was long ago now
in spring.
It was the clematis—
something about the way
it climbed up the trellis,
opening its star-shaped face to the world …

but it's gone now,
the poem or whatever it was
that prompted the momentary pause,
the reflection that gives birth to words.

I want to blame it on the baby.
Ever since his birth,
the world's been dizzy
with my attending him

and those momentary flickers
of that vastly familiar terrain
which is inspiration
seem snuffed out
by his presence,
his cheeky impudence.

I'm the poem, he says.
Look at me!
And he holds up his hand,
star to my face.

Thirst

In the dark hours of the night,
my daughters stirs beside me
and asks for a cup of water.

I grumble and groan.

Get it yourself.

She asks again,
I'm thirsty, Mommy.
Please. It's dark.

*

The light in the bathroom is dazzling.
The water runs out of the tap
in a noisy stream.

I fill her cup.

She drinks,
and is satisfied.

*

When I return to the dark,
I cannot sleep.

Prayer comes to my lips
as it always does in hours like this.

Lord. Lord, I thirst.

Thumbsucker

Spring, a time for lost mittens—
the casual stray left on an old snowbank,
hung up on a twig, or lying sodden in the alley.

My daughter, the thumbsucker,
has lost a mitten. Once again.

The eye traverses the sky, looking for
that break in the clouds, the swift rise in temperature
that signals the season's arrival.

And then, a quick glance to the ground.

Oh where, oh where, has that mitten gone?

In her stroller, my daughter sucks
to soothe herself into sleep;
her other hand is the sound of one hand's clapping,
silent applause to enduring habits of childhood long forgotten.

Going backwards in our travel,
to find the lost colour of her hands, my hair wisps with white
—late snow dusting the land with a mother's worry.

It is just a lost mitten.
When will she ever stop sucking her thumb?
How will I ever find it now?

When I return she is asleep, mouth agape,
thumb off to the side. Silver light
falls across her face and for a moment,
she is fallen cherub, fallen time
in the brief season of a mother's gaze.

Wild Blueberries

Someone has hauled these
through the dark night
down a lonesome stretch
of northern Ontario highway.

By the time they reach the table
where my toddler's hands pick and fumble
to bring their sweetness into her mouth,

they are well-travelled souls.

All I can think of
is the rumble of midnight
and the star-shine that carried them these
few hours before the market's opening.

How they were gleaned
from wooded fields by strange hands
and kept cool in a box
shaded by trees.

Blue, sweet tender night,
your passing has never brought
a more succulent treasure than these—

night sky's dark gems
glistening in the morning light.

Ripen

Tomatoes ripen on the windowsill,
deep green bruising into red;
each one different in the way flesh takes to fire.

Cut off, their stems withered from the frost,
all change must now come from within.

Rotund aspect of the soul, plump-bitter
from having been severed too soon, it will muster
its own sun to burnish the skin.

My eyes await their transformation, as God must
in looking on, pure light affixing to each fruit
as if on a sparrow, a hair on the head—a gaze
that yearns and is made captive, waiting
for an aria about to unfold from the green throat
soon to avenge its early plucking.

The Children's Teeth

come erupting out of the gum, plinths and pillars
of ivory stonehenge around the god suntongue
that flaps and trills wordnoise to name the world
and itself. *There's no controlling where they'll go,*
the dentist says to worried mother before the child's
first trip to the orthodontist. *The spacing of one's teeth*
depends entirely on what grows in beside it
or what refuses to come out. The playground
of the mouth is all teeth have, the molar's peer
jostling the other like a bully. Sometimes one just
has to come out when they huddle or crowd too much,
the silver pliers descending—*deus ex machina*—
on the recalcitrant unable to leave gummy ground.
Ka-Ching! The tooth lands on the metal dish shaped like a kidney,
and suddenly, there is more room in the bed of the mouth,
and the little ones left there grow bold into the space now made
for them. *Teeth are a kind of family,* the dentist says,
but sometimes they need to be jerked around a little to fit in.
Like words in a poem, he adds, and gives a smile
as crooked as an upside-down frown.

Bitch-Self

Sometimes when the anger surges through,
you become *her*—dog mother, the snap and snarl moment
at the whelp, wanting to bite its ass, *the little shit!*
Bitch-self you become—
overwhelmed by fatigue and frustration—
dog hours measured in Prufrock spoons.

Mothering sometimes is just badass work.

Wipe the spill, wipe their bums, wipe their noses,
along with wipe the counter, wipe the toilet, wipe the floor;
every moment of it is a down-at-the-heels one—
No wonder they're crying the blues, those little dog-eared
tabs of misery in the book you'll never finish
for the interruptions! Some days, there are no
ways of getting away from it, the dog dish with its
heap of jumbled-up bones, when you have to stoop,
lower your head to eat it. Some say, this is the destiny
your body was born for while you, you'd rather just
yip at the moon.

About Her Hysterectomy

Good riddance to the womb, she tells me in a letter, that wee pocket
of shrivelled flesh in between the hips, the inner sanctum
of that once capacious abode now become back shed.

It pains her, dully, as sometimes the children who came from there do
in that opaque offensive way children have of taking "home"
for granted.

Still around, they have not flown the coop but peck
at one another while her wings have long worn out
from too much sheltering, too much flapping about.

There will be no more.
Children, that is.
And the pain, too, she figures.

For the womb is like a cupped hand, holding water,
leaking time, muscles' hourglass expanding and contracting.
Breathing in gestational mortal gasps, its purpose
is of fixed time and place.

When the water has been drunk,
the hand goes slack, and everything it was meant to contain
now dribbles back to the source.

She who has laboured to meet her thirst
is finished, and her body wants none of it.

Perambulator

Casement of wonder, carapace of the helpless eye,
this mother-wheeled travelling sideshow from another era
idles by the dumpster, awaiting destruction.

Babyless, it is derelict.

How many infants coasted on those
now rusted wheels, their round faces turned up to sun and sky
as the springs juddered them over sidewalk and pavement?
Bonnetted and cossetted, all eye and ear, they were once
pure observer, launched by the lovely-limbed creature
all milk and sustenance, caress and devotion.

Now, she who strode the earth with them is gone,
the body husked, the shell empty, laid aside,
and the wonder that remains is in glassy pools of rain
and fallen leaf, dew and odd bits of debris
cobwebbed, cradled, and awaiting the end.

Frightened

My mother, an old woman,
watches the news
three times a day.
Each time there are war planes
on the screen
she stares, transfixed.

When they came at night, she said,
they roared like thunder
pouring incendiaries from their bellies
like a string of pearls, light unstrung.

She and her sister ran to the shelter,
huddled there in silence
until it was over.

She was ten years old.

Once during a particularly awful raid,
my grandmother, baby strapped onto her back,
took all her children, running, to their uncle's;
banging on the warehouse door, she begged to be let in,
but he couldn't help them, because the rest
of the neighbourhood was huddled in there already.

"That was when she found us a place in the country,"
Mother said, of her mother. "Father, you see,
was away at war."

Now, when she watches those children on TV,
their anxious faces soon to cast glances skyward,
I cannot tell if she is mother or child,
whether she is remembering the fear,
or the love.

A Church-going Mother Contemplates the Buses in London

In this city of churches, there are buses with signs
that say "There is probably no God."

People are carried by this probability, the way platelets
flow in a stream of plasma to all the major organs
of the body.

This blood is indifferent to its travels;
that there will always be an end, a place to step off onto the
pavement, is a faith implicit in the hardness of things.

My oldest son will not ride the buses with these signs.
He thinks them blasphemous. He does not trust the driver.

I hold his hand at the stop. And wait for one
that is not so offensive.

We see the steeple of our destination from far away
and we cannot get there, because he is obstinate, resolute.

When I think of my need to get there, I am tempted
to think of *need* as a graven image; the bus sign chastening me
for my old-fashioned weakness for belief.

I think of the opium I need to smoke in the pew, the incense
that fills the nostrils like a soporific.

Weakness is the smoked mirror I see through darkly,
hope the substance in its depths.

It is then I cling to my son's hand like a woman in fear for her life
and am grateful that he is mine; and if indeed he is all I have,
that is plenty enough, to believe.

Childhood

Everything about it speaks to its impermanence—
curling ends of boxboard stars, spilled glitter in the vents,
chewed lollipop sticks, chocolate on the face,
moist sphere of the bubble.

The body lives the sensations only once
        with a mind too small to know the significance,

and yet what finer tableau to print upon the surface—
        the flight of birds, time passing
in that magnanimous sweep of wings against
        season-altered skies.

Our ambition out of it propels
        the suckling mouth to form words—
soldiers marching out of the maw
        of unknowing, transformed as young men are
when they know they must die—
words to command the world, to beckon it
with names. Soon they form the garrison
        of a growing consciousness that seeks
to stay the crayon sun and moon
        from its passage across papered skies,
that presses back the curling ends of pointed stars,
        and keeps their glitter in a jar.

        It happens so swiftly,
this marathon of days—the length of a wisp of grass—
because it ends, and ends again each time we look back at what it was
to have tasted sweetness in the mouth
        from the salt of our remembering.

Nostalgia

Eye-tunnel of memory, tracking like searchlights, morsels of time
to prey on. When caught, the motes are illumined and become
snowflake-sharp, tines like knives, crystalline, caught in a
beaker solution of gaze and absolve. When like two doves,
memory and word, they settle on a portion of stilled time, they
become feathered nest, a place for the soul to repose, egg-like
in its charm. Everywhere such sight alights, it wishes to linger,
but cannot. As flight in birds is natural to creatures feathered and
winged, so too, the human longing for hidden time, in which a
moment might hang, an ornament of grace, a diamond in the air
waiting like fruit to be plucked and savoured.

Notes on the Poems

"Trumpet" and its counterpoint poem "O Magnum Mysterium" were commissioned for CBC Radio on a series they did on poetry and music. Charles Ives' "The Unanswered Question" is a short orchestral piece that philosophically explores "The Perennial Question of Existence" with the use of a trumpet, woodwinds and strings. Tomás Luis de Victoria's "O Magnum Mysterium" is a Latin choral piece that manifests medieval Christianity's sense of awe and reverence at the miracle of Christ's birth.

Italicized lines in "Little Gidding—In Homage" are from T.S. Eliot's poem "Four Quartets." See http://www.tristan.icom43.net/quartets/.

The epigraph to "Boomerang" is from P.K. Page's *The Glass Air* and is used with permission.

"Poetry" is for Tim Bowling, who once mentioned to me that poetry was "a discipline of consciousness"—which got me thinking about poetry in a new way. Thanks, Tim.

The epigraph to "Poet" is from Jean-Michel Basquiat, an American expressionist artist who died tragically young at the age of 28 in 1988. Basquiat made remarks about art which are often quoted, and it is from a website of his "quotables" that I discovered this one. See: http://www.artquotes.net/masters/basquiat-quotes.htm

Scripture quoted on pages 48 and 58 is from the *King James Version Bible*. Scripture quoted on pages 7, 11, 22, 42, and 61 is from *New Revised Standard Version Bible* and is used with permission.

Some poems in this collection with some or no alteration have been previously published. "Alert to Glory" appeared in *Language for a New Century* published by Norton in 2008. "Ducks" and "Blueberries" appeared in *A/Cross Sections: New Manitoba Writing* published by the Manitoba Writers' Guild, Winnipeg, Manitoba in 2007. "Creator Destroyer" appeared in *Drunken Boat* (Winter 2010)."Caress" and "Bisque" appeared in *The New Quarterly* (Fall 2008)."Spring Break," "Poets out of Stones" and "God the Tea Master" appeared in *Event* (Fall 2008). "Clematis" appeared in *The Malahat Review* (Fall 2000).

Acknowledgements

A special thanks to editors Sharon Caseburg and Allan Briesmaster for their fine work on *Alert to Glory*. Thanks also to the Manitoba Arts Council, which provided funding for work on the manuscript.

Thanks also to Sumiko Shirai and Michiko Tsuboi, who helped with the translation of the title poem so that the cover art could be designed by Gen Tsuboi, kiri-e artist and designer based in Kyoto, Japan. *Domo arigato gozaimashita.*

Thanks also to fellow poets Don Domanski, Fiona Lam, Joanne Epp, Sarah Klassen for their friendship, support and encouragement along this path to publication.

And finally love and gratitude to family—my husband, Paul Dyck, my children, Kenji and Seika—whose daily presence and levity of mind are much appreciated.